D0716726

A PIECE OF THE QUIET

PAUL WILSON

INSTANT PEACE AND QUIET
FOR A NOISY, NON-STOP WORLD

MACMILLAN

Pan Macmillan Australia

in paperback 2008 by Macmillan
an Macmillan Ltd
Vharf Road, London N1 9RR
.e and Oxford
s throughout the world
nacmillan.com

-0-230-01607-1

Calm Centre Pty Ltd 2006
ht © Wendy Blume 2006

ilson to be identified as the
author of this work has been asserted by him in accordance
with the Copyright, Designs and Patents Act 1988.

1 3 5 7 9 8 6 4 2

A CIP catalogue record for this book is available from
the British Library.

Cover design by Niccola Phillips

Printed and bound in Great Britain by
Butler & Tanner, Frome

Visit **www.panmacmillan.com** to read more about all our books
and to buy them. You will also find features, author interviews and
news of any author events, and you can sign up for e-newsletters
so that you're always first to hear about our new releases.

Carry a piece of the quiet.
Concentrate on silence. When it comes, dwell on how it sounds.
Then strive to carry that quiet with you wherever you go.

The Little Book of Calm

This book will help you find peace of mind whenever you feel the need.

It contains dozens of practical ways to produce a little inner quiet when times get tough. And to get more out of life when times are great.

But the best part about it is there's no waiting.

You probably have too many things on your plate as it is. Far too busy to want to take on new disciplines or practices. So this book works in an á la carte fashion: 'Today I'll have a bit of this; maybe a dash of that.'

Ignore the fact that there is order in the way the pages flow. This book is at its most useful when you allow it to work with you. Open it at random whenever you feel the urge. Whatever page is in front of you is the best place to start.

Then, all you have to do to find some peace and quiet is to let go, and follow where your intuition leads.

Before the Peace and Quiet

Imagine how good it would feel if you could go out into the street right now and see that the world had been transformed.

Instead of the tense and troubled place you saw on the news last night, you now see one that's harmonious and calm. Instead of the cold and uncaring bear-pit you've had to compete in each day, you find one that's carefree and considerate. Instead of congestion, you find space. Instead of noise and information overload, you find quiet.

In short, instead of restlessness, you find peace of mind.

It can be like this.

Sounds extraordinary, but you can be enjoying the peace and quiet in no time.

In the next few pages you will discover that this is not some utopian dream you have to struggle for. It's just a state of mind. One that you can turn on or off by directing your attention in a certain way.

Bite-sized peace of mind

There's a school of thought that says ongoing peace of mind as I've just described it is for the privileged few. Long-term meditators, for example.

While it's true that practices such as meditation make it easier to live with the noise and pressures of modern life, there are other ways as well.

Some are more immediate.

A Piece of the Quiet presents a range of these.

They'll enable you to enjoy many of the benefits that long-term meditators experience, but without having to put in all the training and effort.

In fact many of the suggestions ahead are based on shortcuts that long-term meditators intuitively use, but which aren't part of traditional training.

Use them occasionally and you can make your immediate world more peaceful. Use them regularly and you'll find that your thinking is clearer, your emotions lighter and more stable, and your overall state of wellbeing is enhanced. The external pressures and tensions will still be there, of course, but you'll have the resources to diminish their impact.

Four ways to peace and quiet

As you go through these pages you'll see four different symbols. They apply to the approach you might take to the practice or attitude on that page.

Let's start with the obvious one – the rational or intellectual approaches. These everyday skills and strategies are identified by this wide-awake symbol:

Sometimes the suggestions will take you further.

Now it becomes a bit less intellectual, and slightly more experiential. Now your body is feeling more relaxed, even though you're still alert and focused. As you can tell from this symbol:

But you can go further still. Like slipping out of gear and into neutral. Just idling. Your thoughts are slower and more relaxed. Less intense, but still focused. Notice how this is making you feel even more peaceful?

And then we come to turning off the engine altogether. This will encourage you to stop, and forget about everything that's happening for a moment. Enjoy a deep sense of peace and quiet. It doesn't mean you're asleep or in a trance, but in a state of restful alertness. You will know exactly what it feels like when you see this symbol:

What's the best one for you?

Choose any page at random. Experiment, trust your intuition, and see where it takes you. But keep this book close at hand. This way you'll be able to tap in to the peace and quiet at whim.

PEACE AND QUIET NOW

Why wait? Have it now

We live in an immediate, impatient world. Seems we're always looking forward to the next thing.

But whenever you become too focused on what's ahead (or what has gone before) you miss out on what's going on now.

If you bring your attention to the present – which you can do by letting go of all that's on your mind and focusing on what is before you now – you discover that it is not only more satisfying, but it relieves a host of other pressures.

Take time pressure. When you focus on this moment, time pressure doesn't just diminish, it vanishes completely. Gone. And it can never return as long as your attention remains here.

Take worry and anxiety as another example. As both relate to the future, they simply do not exist when your mind is filled with the present. As well, guilt and regret belong to the past, and cannot be experienced when your attention is on the present.

This moment is all you get. It would be a great pity if you squandered it because you were distracted by something less real.

The only moment you can experience happiness is this one. You can't extract it from the past, that's memory; and you can't bring it back from the future, that's fantasy.

Similarly, the only moment you can experience love is now. You can only experience peace and equanimity now. You can only experience contentment now.

Enjoy them now.

Free for the time being

You can try this as you read this page.

Just for the moment, surrender all of your concerns and responsibilities. Put them to one side. If you really need to, you can come back to them later.

Just for the moment, centre your attention and allow yourself to be relaxed about where you are now.

Just for the moment there is not another thing that needs to be done. In fact, for the time being, you can forget about 'doing' altogether. Now you can concentrate on 'being'. Being here. Being relaxed.

Being present.

Just as there is nothing you have to do, there is nothing you have to think about. No lesson to be learned, and no meaning to be taken. Allow your mind to fill with the experience of this instant. Just being.

If you stop and really devote your attention to it, you discover that this moment is dimensionless. It has no end. You can go on enjoying it as long as you focus here now, and allow things to happen at their own pace.

And it continues until you go back to thinking about the past or the future again.

The most important moment ever

There are all sorts of reasons why you might want to evaluate what's gone by, and plan for what might happen. However, the past and future are fabrications. Neither exist outside of the human mind. If you treat them too seriously, if you pay them too much attention, you miss out on the only opportunity you will ever have to enjoy life.

Which is now.

Life is taking place in this moment only. Nothing is happening in the past. Nothing is happening in the future. Now is all there is. If you think too hard about it, this may seem abstract or theoretical.

But when you practise it, you know it's true.

Practising means throwing yourself into the deep end of whatever is before you – work, pleasure, study, stimulation, eating, meditation – as if this were the only opportunity you will ever have to experience it.

Practising means making the decision to experience life as it is happening. To derive pleasure and satisfaction from everything you do. To treat every moment as if it were the last. It sometimes helps to remind yourself that 'this is the most important moment in my life'.

Don't just think it; actually say the words. 'This is the most important moment in my life.'

Hear yourself saying it now.

Total fulfilment

Have you ever wondered how someone can get satisfaction from performing the same mundane task day in day out, while you squirm at the thought of having to do it for even half an hour?

Is it that you have a lower boredom threshold than they do? Or is it that they know something about work and life that you may not?

You can turn the most mind-numbing chore or activity into something fulfilling and comforting by doing just one thing. Devoting all of your attention to it. Not part of your attention. Or most of your attention.

Devote all of your attention to it.

When you wholly commit yourself to an activity, and immerse yourself in its flow and detail, a transformation takes place.

In no time at all you forget what the task means or represents, and you're absorbed by the process. It's as if it all takes place in a single moment.

This is the most peaceful and harmonious way of approaching any task. It's also intensely satisfying. You discover that ironing a shirt collar is every bit as fulfilling as composing an opera or pulling off a business deal.

And all you're doing is focusing on the present.

Stillness to go

In an ideal world you'd be able to carry about a piece of the quiet that you could call upon when the pressure was on. Could it be that you're living in an ideal world?

The most obvious way you can do this is to use your recollections or imagination. Recall a time in the past when you were peaceful and content. Immerse yourself in the detail. Allow the recollection of those original feelings to change the way you're feeling now.

Notice the difference a simple recollection can make?

A more portable way is to make a practice of being mentally present when you are physically present.

When you're at work, bring all of your attention into the workplace; don't think about shopping, home or dinner tonight.

When you're at home, keep your attention at home.

When you're reading, walking, shopping, sweeping, cooking, eating, mending, tending, sailing, sun-baking or making love, do it with all of your attention.

Being mentally present when you are physically present enables you to experience an equanimity and inner stillness in all types of situations – regardless of how difficult or mundane they may be.

Peace where there's quiet

It's hard to escape the fact that the world is getting noisier.

Even if you discount the physical noise, the emotional and intellectual noise can be deafening. You're exposed to literally thousands of individual messages each day – more than your grandparents would have seen in a year.

And when a gap occasionally does appear, it seems like something's amiss or missing. Somewhere along the line we started to accept – at least on a subconscious level – that all empty spaces should be filled. That stimulation is positive, and that the quiet is somehow negative or less than ideal. And that you shouldn't just sit there, you should do something.

I'd like to suggest the opposite. That rather than doing something, you should just sit there.

And that empty spaces are a godsend.

At a deeper level, you know there's something magical about the quiet. You know this from your moments in the countryside, on the mountaintop, in the rainforest or the temple.

And you know it from those blissful, twilight moments just as you're about to fall asleep at night.

When you make a practice of bringing some of this quiet into your day – even if it's only for a minute or so at a time – you progressively overcome the feeling of restlessness and unease that seems to define our age.

Just a bit of the quiet is all it takes.

In the space of 10 minutes

The conventional line of thinking is that quiet is the space between sounds. Other people tend to think of it as the space in which sounds arise. Either way, it's a space.

Whether it's physical, mental, chronological or aural, space leads to peacefulness. Here's how you can find some without stepping outside your door.

It's a pleasant little mental time-out you can do in just 10 minutes – the time it takes to make a cup of tea and drink it. It's made even more powerful if you do it twice a day.

What you have to do during this time is ... nothing at all. No need to meditate, adopt yoga positions or visualise. Just sit there. Be content to do nothing, without feeling there is anything that has to be done.

Just be for 10 minutes.

The art is to resist the urge to occupy the space. Resist the urge to look at your watch. Resist the urge to perform those little mental chores you've been putting off. Resist the urge to feel guilty about doing nothing.

Accept that there's nothing you have to think about, nothing you have to do, no right or wrong way of doing it. Just sit and be happy to be idle.

Before you know it, the peace of mind and feeling of spaciousness you experience in this innocent little 10-minute practice will have spread to other parts of your day.

As peaceful as you can imagine

If you could be transported to a wide open field or a deserted beach right now, you'd instantly feel more peaceful. You also feel more peaceful if you do this entirely in your imagination.

Even though it is future-based, and takes you out of the present, what you imagine has a powerful effect on what you feel.

Use it to feel some peace of mind now.

There was a time in your past when everything fell into place. Maybe it involved a particular setting – a mountaintop, a secluded island, a rainforest, a gently flowing stream, the seaside, an old church, a remote temple, a quiet corner of your house.

Maybe it's pure fantasy – a place you'd love to visit, or an experience you'd love to have.

Maybe it was the company – a lover, a parent, a child in your arms. It may have been a line of poetry. Or an inspired artistic or athletic performance. Or an act of heroism or survival.

The place or the event doesn't really matter. All that's important is the feeling that it brings to mind.

Close your eyes and allow your imagination to run with it now …

What do you think it looks like? The colours, textures, the time of day. What are your surroundings? What are you wearing? What is the expression on your face?

Don't try to force the image. Let it come if it's going to; otherwise, just pretend that you can see it.

Now turn your attention to what you can hear. The applause, the music, the birds, the children's voices. You might be able to hear your own breathing. Does it sound slower, more relaxed than usual?

Now turn your attention to what you can taste or smell. The salt on your lips. The smell of roses or perfume.

It's almost as if you are there. The more sensory detail you call, the more real it will be.

Now, with all of these sensations in mind, turn your attention to what you feel.

Feel the tingle down your spine as the curtain rises. The warmth of the sun on your face, the snow beneath your feet, the breeze against your back, the hardness of the chair, the tenderness of the touch.

Hold on to that feeling.

Between one word and the next

Ever noticed the number of words that flow through your mind?

Even when none actually passes your lips, it's estimated that you subvocalise hundreds of words per minute – more or less echoing everything you think about, plan to do, or recall.

By any measure, this amounts to a lot of mental chatter.

If there was a way of adding a little space between those words, it would have the effect of slowing down your thoughts. This automatically leads to a more restful state of mind.

There are many ways of doing this, but the easiest also happens to be one of the most effective. All you have to do is add the word 'space' to your inner vocabulary.

Every time you breathe out, imagine hearing this one word: 'Space.'

Imagine hearing it in your own voice. Keep hearing it. Over and over.

As quirky as this seems, it eases the internal chatter, reduces the number of words, and creates space for a tranquil state of mind.

Peace of mind in a body

It's commonly believed that the path to peace of mind involves a lot of mental effort or discipline. 'If only I could stop myself thinking sometimes.' 'If only I could make myself relax.' 'If only I could force those thoughts out of my mind.'

But history's most influential shamans, salespeople and hypnotists have shown us a way that involves much less effort. That is, the quickest way to positively influence the mind is to start with the body.

It takes less effort to make a physical change than to make a mental change. It's easier to modify your rate of breathing, for example, than it is to start feeling more relaxed.

Similarly, it takes less effort to implement a mental step than it does to change your state of consciousness.

You'll find it easier to focus your attention on a sound or an object than you will to change from an everyday state to a meditative one.

Simply making a physical change can be an efficient first step in changing your state of consciousness.

Start at the centre

Stay really still for a moment. Withdraw your attention from the outside world, and bring it to a place you feel might be your centre.

This simple feat of imagination brings you squarely into the present. And takes you one step away from the noise and tensions of the day-to-day world.

It also begins to change your mental state. In fact, this began the moment you sensed the stillness within.

Now turn your attention to the ground. Sense where your feet touch the floor. Feel the anchor points beneath each foot. Notice how stable and grounded that makes you feel?

With this in mind, imagine what it would feel like to be suspended by a thread – so that each of your vertebra is able to swing freely, like a long string of beads, coming to rest in the perfect vertical position.

Now your body will be feeling centred, grounded and balanced – from the top of your head to the soles of your feet. You feel stable and secure.

More importantly, your mental state grows more centred and relaxed as you do it.

That's why a centring practice such as this is the first step of most meditation practices.

A *wider perspective*

An effective but little known way of settling your mental state involves how you use your eyes.

You already know one way of doing this, intuitively at least. Just lower your eyelids, or even partially lower them, and you start to feel more restful. A measurable change in your brainwave patterns has begun.

A less obvious way is simply to widen your vision.

That's all you have to do. Allow your peripheral vision to widen so you take in more and more of the room around you. No need to move your eyes or change your focus in any way, just allow your field of view to expand.

As you do this, a number of subtle physiological changes take place. Your brainwave patterns have begun to change, your breathing is slowing, your facial muscles relaxing, and you are becoming progressively more aware of what's going on around you.

And all you've done is widen your peripheral vision.

If for some reason you don't find that to be simple and intuitive, try softening your gaze instead. While this is more visible to an onlooker, it has a similar effect on your mental state.

Just soften your gaze.

A sound far away

It seems counter-intuitive, but you can find relief from the noise and static of the everyday world by just listening. Not to the sounds nearby, but for the sounds far away.

Using your peripheral hearing in this way has a similar effect to using your peripheral vision.

To begin with, it presents a vastly different impression of the world. It also produces a vastly different type of understanding. Instead of being narrow and detailed, it's broad and holistic.

Not only does this enhance your creativity, it makes it easier for you to grasp the big picture.

But its most useful aspect is the way it soothes the nerves and turns off the internal chatter.

Try it now.

Without concentrating in any way, just listen for a sound far off in the distance. Let your attention drift towards it. Notice how everything seems clearer? And how you've automatically started to feel more centred and peaceful?

Just listen.

Breathe as Mother told you

At some stage or another, all meditation traditions have a practice that focuses on breathing.

Not only does this basic action connect you to all living beings on the planet, it's the most obvious and intimate biological function in your life. You live with it from the moment you're born until the moment you die.

However, the reason most spiritual, artistic, sporting, yoga and martial-arts traditions emphasise breathing skills is that they represent one of the quickest ways of changing your physical state, your mental state, even your state of consciousness.

And best of all, you already have the skills: you've been practising them since the moment you were born.

The first step is to do what Mother told you to do when you were tense and needed to relax. Just take a deep breath.

But rather than concentrating on the upper part of your body – with your shoulders rising and your chest swelling – focus lower. Place your hands just below your navel, and feel exactly where your focus should be.

Imagine drawing the air into the base of your lungs. Your hands will feel your stomach rise as you breathe in.

Practise breathing this deeply when you're relaxed, and you'll soon have a powerful calming habit that can be employed at any time.

With the hint of a smile

A Qigong master I used to know would encourage his students to meditate with the hint of a smile on their face. Psychotherapists sometimes urge patients to do similar.

Combined with other methods, this 'hint of a smile' enhances the relaxing effect you experience.

Firstly for psychological reasons. Since the earliest age, you've associated the smile with feeling good.

In addition, you have spent all the years up until now making that association more powerful still. Every time you smile at something pleasant, you reinforce this.

The hint of a smile also works for physiological reasons.

It relaxes all the facial muscles, which in turn causes other muscles in the body to start feeling more relaxed.

You can do it now.

When you subtly feel the corners of your mouth turning up, just a little – as you probably feel the urge to do as you read about it here – you are stimulating the pleasure centres of your brain.

This sets off a range of neurological and physiological events that automatically lead to feelings of happiness and optimism. Whether this was your intention or not.

That's something to smile about, isn't it?

GETTING TO THE POINT

One of the major discoveries of over 6000 years of meditation practice is that the simplest way to clear the mind of uninvited thoughts is to focus on only one thing.

After a minute or so of this you feel your body relaxing, your breathing slowing, and you actually start to enjoy the focusing.

Firstly, because focusing on one thing limits extraneous thoughts. In no time at all, your mind is clear and uncluttered.

Secondly, because your brain plays a wonderful trick on you. As a survival mechanism over the eons, it learned to filter out 'unnecessary' information in your field of attention. So you are fully aware of the sabre-tooth tiger creeping up on you, but hardly notice the landscape it's coming from. You are more aware of the foreground than the background, the moving than the static, the well-defined than the diffuse, and the bold than the subtle. So anything static or constant is eventually filtered out.

If you focus on a single object, action, feeling, word, phrase or action – as you do in some meditative practices – eventually it ceases to register. Just like the hum of the air-conditioner in your office. In effect, you clear everything from your field of awareness – extraneous thoughts as well as what you were focusing on.

What you're left with is far from being a blank, unconscious state. It's pure, unadulterated awareness. The most powerful, creative, yet serene state of consciousness possible for a human to experience.

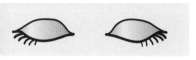

One word is all it takes

You may be familiar with word- or phrase-based meditation practices. In some traditions, the word or phrase you use is known as a mantra.

Some say a mantra has special spiritual vibrations; others say that it invokes the divine; and others say it's just a bunch of words or sounds that may or may not have some historic significance.

Choose any pleasant-sounding word, phrase or sound that takes your fancy, and you'll find that it will work for you. If 'ohm' has no appeal to you, try 'quietly', or 'ocean', or 'marshmallow'.

Give it more meaning if you wish. Choose a prayer, a poem, or a pressure-relieving affirmation like 'I have all the time in the world'.

Bring all of your attention to it.

Imagine the words being said in your own voice. Over and over.

When thoughts come – which they will – gently bring your attention back to this sound.

In a few minutes your mind will be clear, and you'll be feeling peaceful and relaxed. Extend this practice a few minutes more, and you'll be meditating.

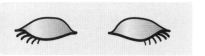

Calm you can count on

Hypnotists and anaesthetists use a similar technique: 'Count back from 10 and you'll feel your body relaxing. Ten, nine, eight – are you feeling sleepy? – seven, six ...' You know the story.

Counting the other way works wonders as a concentrative technique for producing deeply restful, but alert, states.

All you have to do is listen closely to the sound of your breath – as you breathe out – and count each breath.

Breathe in. Now hear 'one' on the out breath. Just imagine you can hear it being breathed in your own, very quiet voice.

Breathe in. Now hear 'two' on the out breath.

Continue for 10 breaths, then start again.

Keep repeating this count for a few minutes and a real change will be taking place. Your mind will be clearing, as your body is relaxing.

This simple practice works in all kinds of environments, from regular meditation sittings to stressful workplaces. Better still, you can do it sitting, standing, walking or even, dare I say it, during boring speeches or presentations.

A picture of equanimity

While dividing your attention causes unrest, focusing it on only one thing produces equanimity, a still frame of mind.

What you focus on is not all that important. While some meditation schools suggest something audible – like a sound, word or phrase – others encourage you to focus on the visual. An image or physical object. This can be meaningless, such as a candle flame; meaningful, such as a sacred image; fantastic, such as in a visualisation; or completely abstract, such as a mandala.

With your eyes partially closed, and your vision soft and relaxed, direct your attention towards this object.

Observe it with fascination. Let all other observations fade. And remember to blink in the usual way.

Observe only the object. Not what it means, nor what it's made from, nor its aesthetics. Just the object.

When thoughts come along, instead of resisting them, observe them passing. Then gently bring your attention back to what's before you. Soon your attention will be filled with the image alone.

Inner quiet in action

It's often believed that to really attain a state of inner quiet, you need to be still and reflective, maybe sitting or even lying down.

But you can produce the same results in a more dynamic way.

You may find direct physical action is a more convenient path to a restful frame of mind if you love the physical side of life, or when you feel under intense pressure and need to expend energy.

Most repetitive activities that you continue for 20 minutes or so will still your thoughts and help you to relax – as long as you're working within your physical capabilities and are not distracting yourself in any way.

You can do this through running, walking, swimming, cycling, rowing, tai chi or dance when you commit totally to the process.

All of the things you normally take for granted about this activity you now observe with fascination. The physical movement of each arm and leg. The feeling beneath your foot as it touches the path and rolls forward. The brush of fabric against your thigh. Just be aware of these sensations as they come and go.

Then you discover that peace and joy are in the activity itself, not where you do it, or its purpose, or its result.

WITH ALL OF YOUR MIND

While concentrative styles of meditation settle the mind by narrowing the attention and emptying it of thought, the same can be achieved by maintaining a more observant state of awareness.

Mindfulness enables you to be fully aware of everything you do or encounter – from your physical self to your mental self to what you are experiencing – so that you can embrace every moment of life.

You might start by observing a specific aspect of your being: your breathing, physical sensations, emotions, even your thoughts. You do this without judgement or analysis. Bit by bit you expand it to take in all aspects of your day – every sip of tea, every detail of your work, every word of conversation, every waft of breeze. Always in the moment they occur.

And when those times come where judgement and analysis are required, you make them activities of the present – to be approached and experienced with mindfulness.

The more you practise this, the more you begin to intuitively appreciate the natural flow of life. Moods, emotions, aches and circumstances are transient; they arise, they fade. You intuitively understand that it's pointless to fear them, cling to them, or identify with them in any way.

Now you're ready to discover that life offers infinitely more opportunity for enjoyment and appreciation than you would ever have imagined.

When you sit back and observe

How often have you heard that the key to a restful state of mind is to learn to focus your awareness?

Strange, because 'focusing your awareness' is not an activity that comes naturally to most people. While you understand what it means, it's not something that features in your everyday life.

Here's an easy-to-understand, easy-to-apply alternative.

Just observe.

Observe anything at all. Doesn't matter if it's to do with yourself – such as your breathing, your feelings, or even your thoughts – or with your surroundings, a sound or an object.

Just observe.

And if you observe in a completely neutral way, without analysis or comparison, something remarkable takes place.

You not only become more mindful of what you're experiencing in that particular moment, but your thoughts start to slow, distractions cease, and you progressively ease into a restful, maybe even meditative state.

And all you have to do is observe.

Rising and falling in total awareness

If you narrow your attention to the most elementary aspect of your being – your breathing – you are never more than a few breaths away from a peaceful, harmonious state.

Take it further and bring your attention to the total act of breathing, and you not only train the awareness to remain in the present, you gain a powerful insight into the natural flow of life.

Imagining yourself in the centre of the breathing experience, observe one breath as it becomes another.

With eyes closed, or your gaze softly focused slightly in front of your nose, feel the cool air flowing in – somewhere near the edges of your nostrils. Be aware of the most subtle sensations.

Now when you breathe out, notice how the flow seems slightly different.

Once you are comfortable with the inflow and outflow, broaden your attention so you're aware of how breathing influences other parts of the body.

Note the subtle rise and fall of your chest. The contraction and expansion of your rib cage. The tensing and the release of your diaphragm. The subtle rise and fall of your shoulders.

That's all there is to it. Just keep observing. Soon you'll not only be relaxed, you'll be enjoying a state of alertness that's untouched by the movement of thought or distraction.

Feel this if you dare

Your moods and emotions colour your view of the world. If you're nervous, everything is threatening. If you're depressed, everything is bleak. If you're in love, everything is rosy. If you're relaxed, all is peaceful.

Usually, what you're feeling is beyond your direct control. Try to resist an unpleasant feeling, and you increase its sting. Try to hold on to a pleasant one, and it transforms into something else.

But if you experience your feelings mindfully, you discover just how transient your emotions and mental states are. The instant you become aware of them, they begin to change. Restlessness becomes irritation or anger. Anger becomes fear or guilt. Guilt becomes tenderness or love.

When you place yourself at the very centre of what you're feeling, you become more objective about it.

You discover that a pleasant or positive feeling only exists in the moment that it occurs. That suffering is not caused by any negative feeling, but by how you respond to it. And that your emotions and mental states do not define you.

Accepting this at the deepest level is a certain way to achieve peace of mind.

Where did that thought go?

Although thoughts can be intrusive when you're trying to relax and slow down, the best way to treat them is with indifference. 'It's a thought. That's nice. Now back to the relaxing.'

While we often think in terms of one thought, or a single thought, the nature of thinking is motion.

Thoughts are always coming and going. One arises, links with another, and a process is in train. The only time they become intrusive is when you engage them.

Treat thoughts with indifference, and they'll pass without involving you in any way.

Think of them as you would a flow of people past your window.

They appear and they pass in their own good time, but you have no influence or direct involvement with them.

Observe with your full attention if you like, but only in the moment they're passing through.

Then relax and let them go.

The practice of work

What a blessing it would be if, instead of seeing your work as a chore or a duty, you could savour it as a way of practising mindfulness. A way of extracting every gram of satisfaction from your working day. A way of finding peace of mind.

Millions of people do this every day.

When you undertake a task with your full attention – taking care to perform every aspect of it to the best of your capabilities, and not trying to distract yourself with unrelated thoughts or stimulation – you derive an unusually high level of satisfaction from what you do. Even if it's a task you would normally get no pleasure from.

It's just a matter of being fully occupied with what is before you. If you're filing papers, you do it with your total attention. As if at that moment, nothing else exists. Same when you're cooking dinner, washing the car, or painting the laundry.

When you work this way, time flies, you perform with greater efficiency, and you feel centred and fulfilled at the same time.

And if you make a practice of being mindful in your daily life, all work becomes a pleasant way of clearing all those unwanted thoughts and producing a peaceful state of mind.

WITHOUT EFFORT

The first great turning point in life is when you realise how little of it you can control.

You have no control over big things like the universe, the climate and the economy. And you have no control over the little things like your immediate surroundings or your subordinates.

Even the domain that you believe you have most influence over – yourself – is beyond your direct control. You can't control your health, your heartbeat, your moods or even your thoughts.

In fact the more you believe you can do this, and the more effort you apply, the less you achieve. Try to control life's natural ebb and flow, and you end up frustrated. Try to control others, and you end up disappointed. Try to force yourself to relax or slow down, and you end up tense. Try to force yourself to stop thinking a certain way, and you become even more committed to that line of thinking.

All you can effectively control is your urge to control things.

The moment you do this, you feel free. It's the same sense of freedom you feel when you sail with the wind rather than rowing against the current. When you use your opponent's strength and momentum in a martial art. When you stop squinting into the darkness, and put your faith in your peripheral vision.

You also feel this sense of freedom in processes of the mind, such as meditation. The greatest rewards come when you surrender control, and just be.

Do nothing and go deeper

When you're wanting to take your state of relaxation to a deeper level, you arrive at a stage where you realise everything is beyond your control – and there's not a single thing for you to manage or direct, and nothing you can do to add to the process.

You start to appreciate the paradox that your efforts are most effective when you apply no effort. And you encourage peacefulness when you step back and allow it to arrive in its own way, in its own good time.

Allow yourself to do nothing for a few moments, and you will experience how this works.

Observe how liberating it feels when you allow things to happen at their own pace.

Observe how it feels to let go of your need to be doing, and how much more fulfilling it is just being.

Being here.

Being present.

Being relaxed.

No eye on the outcome

In this achievement-oriented age, it may seem unnatural or even undesirable to participate wholeheartedly in something without being fully aware of where you're headed and having an outcome firmly in mind.

Yet when it comes to inner achievements like relaxing and letting go, that's exactly what is required.

Because in matters of the mind – whether it be relaxation, understanding, remembering, creativity, emotion, intuition – the less effort you apply, the greater the result. Only when you forget about outcomes and focus on the present can you achieve the most peaceful states.

This even applies to areas of physical achievement. The best results come when you plan where you want to end up, then concentrate all of your attention on putting it into effect.

Only when outcome is out of your mind can you relax and enjoy the process.

Beyond effort and analysis

When you sit quietly, let go of the outside world, and give in to a state of quiet alertness, an extraordinary process begins.

As long as you don't try to influence what's happening, your muscles will be relaxing.

All of them.

As long as you don't expect anything in particular to happen, your vision will be softening. Just a little.

And your breathing will be sounding more relaxed.

As long as you don't think about what's happening, your mind will be clearing of uninvited thoughts. And as long as you don't try to analyse what is happening or compare it with anything else, your mental state will be becoming more settled.

More peaceful.

All this at the same time as you remain wide awake and alert.

You can continue to enjoy this feeling as long as you do so ... without analysis, without expectation, and without effort.

Allow me to help you feel peaceful

A sure way to change your state of consciousness from the everyday to the deeply relaxed is to hand over responsibility to somebody else.

So instead of you taking the steps required to make the change, you simply follow the guidance of another. You can do it here, now. Without doing another thing, you can suspend control for a moment as you take on the suggestions ahead. And allow them to lead you into a pleasant state of relaxation that requires no effort on your part.

First, let's see if you can recall a place where you always find it easy to feel peaceful and relaxed.

For a few moments, put aside your analytical thoughts, and return to that place. As you do this, try to imagine the look on your face as you re-experience its peacefulness.

An onlooker would see an expression that may be much more serene than you can imagine.

What you are discovering is that just by imagining you are in a calm and restful place, you are becoming calm and restful. Even if you can't imagine yet what an onlooker might see, your physiology is changing. As long as you relax and go along with the suggestion, all signs of tension are fading … facial muscles becoming relaxed … jaw and forehead following … maybe the hint of a smile forming on your lips.

You should see the peaceful look on your face right now.

When you least expect it

We expect a lot in life. We expect it of ourselves, our friends, the government, fellow drivers and public figures.

However, this can only ever deliver a variation on what you are expecting. Not only does this blind you to the beauty of everything else there to enjoy, but it commits you to a certain outcome: 'When X happens, I expect Y to be the result. When I do good, I expect good in return.'

This influences every aspect of your life.

Whether you apply it consciously or unconsciously, it involves an effort to exert control. It creates an emotional attachment to an outcome.

While this has a role to play in certain parts of life – for example, you expect oncoming traffic to be driving on the correct side of the road – it can also lead to stress and frustration.

For example, expectations that fail to be realised lead to disappointment. If this happens a number of times, it can lead to resentment. If it applies to other people's attitudes or behaviour, it can lead to hurt or disillusionment. If it occurs in your relationships, it can place them under strain.

But put your expectations on hold, and you are free to appreciate every moment of your day and relationships – no matter how they unfold.

Well, what did you expect?

Often, the difference between unrest and peace of mind is a factor of what you expect.

Expect a lot, and you'll be regularly disappointed. Have no expectations at all, and you'll find life is rich and full of wonderful surprises.

It can be liberating when you finally accept there's no right or wrong way about the way life unfolds.

It is as it is.

When you accept this, when you can step aside from what you 'know' to be the way things are supposed to happen, it's like being a child again.

You can start to experience every aspect of life with freshness and fascination.

Not only does this add a touch of novelty to the mundane, it reveals so much that you might never have otherwise noticed.

Shed a few now

Expectations are like habits. Once collected, they tend to stick around – unnoticed but influencing every aspect of your outlook.

Fortunately, they're easier to shed. If you are aware of them.

Do an expectation audit of your attitudes and you'll likely discover masses of them. Subtle biases and preconceived notions about processes, people and circumstances.

One way to recognise these is to look out for the habitual use of words like 'should', 'must' and 'supposed to' in your conversation or internal dialogue.

Usually this indicates that some sort of expectation exists.

The word to be most aware of is 'should'. 'He should have complimented my ...' 'The government should have done ...' 'Children should always ...' 'If I work hard all year, I should ...'

When you recognise a pattern of this nature, you can remove much of the expectation in it by varying the expression. Instead of 'They should', try substituting something like: 'It would be much fairer if ...' Yes, they're only words, but they're always working away on your subconscious.

Vary these words, defuse your expectations, and you'll be free to experience all of life with freshness and clarity.

A stroll of no expectation

Even the most mundane aspects of life are influenced by what you expect to happen.

When you walk to the bus stop in the morning, you expect the neighbours' dog to bark as you pass their gate, you expect rush-hour drivers to stop when you cross at the lights, you expect the bus to arrive at 7.52, and you expect old gentlemen to say thank you when you offer them your place in the queue.

Expectations.

Some of them arise from your own experience, and others arise from how you think things ought to be. But all are attempts to determine the future, or to impose your will on the world around you.

Next time you walk, try this: instead of expecting certain things to occur, expect nothing. Remain physically centred as you walk. Feel the cool breeze on your face. Be aware of the texture of the path beneath your feet. Notice the fragrance from the damp shrubs.

And observe everything you encounter with complete neutrality.

If you compare the two ways of walking – one with expectations, one without – you'll discover that a real sense of freedom exists only in the latter.

There's no comparison

Can you imagine being completely happy with something, year in year out, then instantly becoming dissatisfied with it – even though it hadn't changed in any way at all?

This is what happens when you compare.

The home you're renting is absolutely delightful ... until you discover that someone is paying half the rent for a similar one in your street. Or, you have the best job in the world ... until you discover that someone else is being paid more than you for the same work.

Comparison, like expectation, goes hand in hand with discontent. If you continually compare what you have or what you're experiencing, you'll always be tempted by what's bigger, better or brighter.

You are happiest and most content when you value and appreciate the uniqueness of what you are and what you're experiencing – without needing to compare it with anything else.

The best way to do this is to remain focused on the present. The more involved you are in what's happening now, the more you appreciate it for what it is – rather than for what it could be.

THE THOUGHT THAT COUNTS

How many times have you said to yourself: 'No matter how hard I try to relax, I just can't stop thinking'? And even though you have very little direct control over your thoughts – their content, flavour, timing, or even their volume – you can't stop trying.

The key to managing them is simple and counter-intuitive.

The first step is recognising that your thoughts are essentially verbal. At the same time as they are mental activities, they're usually based on words and language: you actually subvocalise everything you're thinking.

The second is that your thoughts are restless and dynamic by nature. You never have just one thought; your mind is always moving from one topic to the next in a largely unpredictable pattern. So while you might start out thinking you feel hungry, you're soon thinking of chocolate bars, then how long it is until lunchtime, your waistline, the fact that you have to go to the bank, that the car brakes need fixing, and so on.

The third understanding relates to the sheer volume of thoughts you have. When you're tense, you may have hundreds of thoughts in a minute. When you're relaxed, you'll have only a fraction of this amount.

The last but most important understanding is that the fewer thoughts you have at the same time as you remain wide awake and alert, the more relaxed you will feel, and the more creative your insights will be.

One instead of many

Thoughts depend on change for their existence. They're always on the move – coming from one place to go to another; moving from one concept on to the next. And, at any given time, there'll be many more than you're probably aware of.

How many? Estimates vary, but most say you have at least 30 to 60 thoughts per minute in your everyday state of mind. If you're feeling tense, this number could double. If you're relaxed, it will halve. If you're really relaxed, it will halve again.

And if you can reduce them to just one thought, you'll be meditating. This is why having one thought is the key to most meditation practices. You focus on only one thing, such as a word, an image, an action or a sound, and this slows the movement of your thoughts.

If you were to try it now – just listen to the sound of your breathing for a moment … not concentrating too hard, just listening with curiosity – you would experience this.

Observe one breath in the moment it occurs. Then the next breath. No comparisons or evaluations are necessary, just observation. If random thoughts come along, bring your focus back to your breathing.

Before you know it, your thoughts will be at rest.

More intriguing than you think

No matter how experienced or focused you are at relaxing and stilling the mind, your reverie will be interrupted by uninvited thoughts.

Instead of trying to circumvent them, you could put them to use.

Rather than trying to force them from your mind, accept them.

Let them pass through uninterrupted. Like images on a movie screen – lots of individual still frames that produce the illusion of continuous movement, but which have no relevance in their own right.

Just like the individual frame in a movie, a thought is a passing event. It will come and go – unless you engage it. If you just observe, without ownership and without responding to it, something amazing happens.

It vanishes without trace.

Thought sit-ups

There's a price to pay for living in a world of high-achievers. Even when you try to let go and relax, perhaps to meditate, you tend to think there's a right way and a wrong way of doing it.

You read the meditation book, follow all the steps, and what happens? Instead of being clear and relaxed, your mind is awash with stuff. You've done everything you believe you were supposed to, and all you achieve is a stream of uninvited thoughts.

Who could blame you if you considered this a failure in some way or another?

On the contrary, thoughts are an integral and essential part of meditation practice. It is in the instant you recognise 'I'm thinking', before turning your attention back to what you were focusing on, that you strengthen your practice.

Think of this as like doing sit-ups. It is the resistance of your body weight that builds your strength, not the actual sitting up. Same with meditation. It is the recognition of uninvited thoughts when they arise – not the avoidance of them – that builds mental stability.

And peace of mind comes more effortlessly from a mind that is stable.

You can't stop a thought

If a certain thought comes into your mind, all the willpower and all the mental effort in the world won't prevent it from happening. In fact you'll probably make things worse.

The only way to consciously change one way of thinking is to substitute another. Because substitution is immeasurably more powerful than willpower or mental effort as an agent of change.

So if you want to escape a particular stream of thought, instead of trying to suppress it, simply turn your mind to something else.

You change one thought by thinking of another.

You avoid a negative feeling by replacing it with a positive one.

You overcome limiting thinking habits by substituting enriching ones.

Just think about something that pleases you more.

THE PLUS AND MINUS OF WORDS

Humans are wordy beings. The way we make sense of what's going on within and around us is not through facts and data, but through words and language.

Where you become most aware of this is through that persistent little voice inside your head.

Maybe you've always thought of this as a metaphor for thinking. But it really is a form of articulation. And you really do express all the thoughts you're having through a physical process known as subvocalisation.

By using words – or internal dialogue – you make sense of the world around you. You label things, categorise them, and evaluate whether they're good, bad or indifferent. So what you think of as thoughts are, in one sense, just words.

All this would be fine except that, as the world gets busier and noisier, this little voice gets carried away. Sometimes it just won't shut up. And the more you long for some peace and quiet, the more it wants to chatter. This is not only a source of irritation in itself, but it's also the single greatest impediment to a restful state of mind.

Find a way of keeping that voice in check, and you've found a path to that elusive peace and quiet.

A floating tongue

Most people think of that 'little voice' inside their head as a figment of imagination. But it's actually a physical expression of what you're thinking – reflected by minute signals in your vocal cords and movements of your tongue.

Recognising that there is a physical component to thinking means you can take physical steps to moderate it.

The simplest way is just to prevent your tongue moving the way it does when you formulate the words your thoughts consist of.

You can curb these movements, and the internal dialogue that accompanies them, just by allowing your tongue to 'float' inside your mouth. Alternatively, allow it to rest against the roof of your mouth, or to press lightly behind your teeth.

This not only slows down or eliminates internal dialogue, it greatly relaxes your lower jaw muscles (as well as the upper jaw and the area around the temples), the places where physical tension tends to concentrate.

So, simply by resting your tongue, you get twice the benefit: you slow down the internal chatter, and you physically relax the body.

Quieting the voice

You can produce a deeply relaxed state at this moment by doing just one thing: stop thinking. The instant your mind comes to rest, your state of consciousness changes, and you start to ease into a meditative state.

But you have already discovered that you can't put an end to thinking through mental effort alone.

This is where words can help.

To a large degree, your thoughts are the same as your mental dialogue – the words or subvocalisations you use to make sense of what's around you. Slow down the chatter and you slow down the thoughts.

Quieten the words altogether and you'll have peace and quiet.

Here's how you do it.

In normal conversation, you speak on the outflow of your breath. Your inner chatter usually follows the same pattern.

So when you focus on the outflow of your breath, you interrupt your inner dialogue. The more you focus on this out-breath, the quieter your thoughts become.

Listen to it now.

Listen to how relaxed you're becoming

Most meditation schools teach a breathing meditation technique somewhere along the line. Usually, the practice involves concentrating on the sound or feeling or rhythm of the breath, which progressively leads to a change in your state of consciousness.

The easiest way to do this is just to listen.

Listen now. Listen for the sound of your breathing. Even if you can't really hear it, listening for it starts a psychological chain-reaction that leads you to feel more relaxed.

You can bring this feeling of relaxation into your physical body when you pay attention to the sound of your out-breath.

Because this is the part of the breathing cycle where your body is most relaxed.

Why? Because it takes physical effort to breathe in, but none to breathe out. It's the release of diaphragmatic tension, the act of letting go.

Listen to the sound of your out-breath, and your body starts to relax. Keep listening, and your mental state relaxes as well.

Verbs for feeling good

As well as being intrusive, your internal dialogue influences your attitudes and the way you feel. Sometimes what you say to yourself goes further than mere dialogue, and becomes instruction.

Then, instead of just being a way of helping you make sense of the world, that little voice starts taking over. It urges you to complete chores, make changes, worry about things, and so on.

'I really should give up smoking.'

'I must paint the bathroom.'

'I have to save up for that holiday.'

Sometimes you even hear yourself muttering these thoughts aloud. 'I have to get that document finished by morning.'

Internal instructions like these are usually based around pressure verbs like 'should', 'must' and 'have to'. These verbs subconsciously add to the pressure you believe you're facing. They create restlessness and tension.

You can eliminate most of that underlying pressure simply by modifying the verbs.

First, listen. Then, substitute.

Listen to the words you use in your external and internal dialogue. Note the pressure verbs. Then replace them with more easy-going expressions.

When you get the urge to say 'have to', try saying 'choose to' instead – and you'll start to feel that you are calling the shots rather than just responding to them.

When you hear yourself saying 'must', try substituting 'can' or 'may' – and you'll immediately start to feel more in control.

Why stop there?

You can take it further and substitute words that actually encourage you to feel a certain way. Use words that suggest you are are relaxed about, or happy, or have a choice, and soon you'll be feeling that way.

The more you use these substitute words in your inner dialogue, the less pressured you'll feel.

And the more you actually articulate them, the more you work them into your conversation, the more pronounced the improvements will be.

Love and reverence

It is no coincidence that the two feelings that are most commonly associated with spiritual activity are love and reverence.

On a purely superficial level, all religions promote love, and many people find the result of religious activity to be feelings of reverence.

But it goes much deeper than this.

In the most profound meditative states, two of the three most commonly reported impressions are feelings of love and feelings of reverence. (The third is the feeling of oneness or unity.) This is not a 'love of' or 'reverence for', just the unattached feeling of love or reverence.

Interestingly, the reverse of this also applies: if you experience a feeling of great love or reverence you will be demonstrating a brainwave activity that's almost identical to that of deep meditation.

So simply by having a deep feeling of love – or reverence – you can enjoy the same peaceful state, and the same benefits, as someone who is deep in meditation.

The spread of love

In the same way that reverence automatically leads to a quiet meditative state, so does having deep feelings of love. Whether these relate to someone close to you, or someone you just admire, the result is the same.

Can you conjure up loving feelings out of the blue? Most people can't. But you can use a simplified version of the Buddhist *metta* meditation to accomplish the same.

All it requires is that you direct loving feelings towards one or more individuals that you care about: a child, lover, partner, parent, teacher or someone you admire.

To begin with, relax and allow your mind to clear.

Picture one person you have deep feelings for. Now, imagine that you are radiating love and kindness towards this person. If it helps, you can allow sentiments like the following to run through your mind: 'I am sending you feelings of love and kindness. I wish for you to be happy, peaceful and at ease.'

Repeat this for other people you care about, and soon you'll be experiencing this deep sense of love and compassion yourself. There's virtually no difference between this and a deep meditative state.

For God's sake, act reverent

If you have a strong belief in God or a supreme entity of some nature, you have a peace-of-mind advantage that can take decades of meditation practice to equal.

Because all you have to do to bring about a profoundly peaceful state is to be aware of yourself as a soul or your spiritual essence, then to envisage yourself in the presence of God, the Infinite, the One, the Universe, Nature or any entity you feel strongly about.

Everything flows from this.

You automatically experience a deep sense of reverence. No technique is required.

No effort is required.

You can just sit there – with nothing more than this state of soul+God awareness – and peace of mind naturally follows.

A PIECE OF THE QUIET NOW

As you've seen, there are many different ways to find peace and quiet.

If you've read through all of this book's approaches in one sitting, you may conclude that there are too many to absorb. That's why it is best to choose one – at random – and see where it takes you. Next time, try another. Sooner or later you'll settle on a few that give you the most satisfaction.

Usually, it does take a few because achieving peace of mind is a lifelong activity, and it's more fun and entertaining when you come at it from many directions. In this instance, lots of smaller steps can be more productive than one big leap.

If you've been experimenting with these on your way through these pages, maybe you've started to realise that it's not always necessary to practise routines, to learn something, or actually to do anything. In fact, peace and quiet begins the very moment you stop doing things … and place yourself in the centre of what's happening as it is happening.

If you like, you can pause now, and experience this. Try it. Just pause.

The beauty of pausing is that it doesn't lead anywhere. It doesn't ask anything of you. There's no right way or wrong way of doing it.

Just pause, and you have endless room to relax and savour what's happening now.

It's even easier if you combine it with a tiny decision: to let go of everything for one moment of your life. Do this, and you realise that all your responsibilities are on hold. Just for the moment.

Then you can let go of your workloads and deadlines. Just for the moment.

Let go of your worries, fears and doubts – they're just fantasies about the future, anyway. Let go of regrets, disappointments and everything to do with the past. Same with your successes and accomplishments, your masks and pretences – they have no role in this moment.

Are you starting to enjoy this? Now you can let go of your expectations. Feel free to enjoy and appreciate whatever is happening, without anticipating anything as a result.

The *final* step is to let go of all that enters your mind. It's okay for your *thoughts* to come and go, and for you to treat them with indifference. Let go of any need to engage them, or to analyse or understand them.

Do *you* sense what's happening here? By letting go of the things that constrain you – just for the moment – you feel a huge weight lift. Even though your mind is still, you enjoy great clarity.

And *you're* still on pause – you haven't done a thing.

There's not another thing you have to do

In the physical world, you usually have to do something in order to achieve a result. When you went to school, you received a similar message about the way you used your brain.

But now that you've decided to enjoy a little peace of mind – or reaching the higher levels of mental and spiritual understanding – the opposite applies.

There is nothing you have to do.

No effort or analysis is required.

No knowledge or comprehension, no sacrifice, no special training or talent is required. No learning is required – in

fact some people find peace of mind arrives when they start unlearning stuff.

There is a great relief that comes from realising that there's nothing you have to do to discover this elusive inner state.

It arises when you stop doing, and start being. When you stop striving towards things and start enjoying where you are.

It takes only the slightest shift of consciousness for this to happen. You let go of the outside world.

You accept that there's no need to analyse or compare. You ease back and allow whatever happens to happen. And you just listen for the quiet.

A quiet inner peace naturally follows.

It's subtle, but precious. And it happens of its own accord.

You may have already noticed it.

It's been here all along.

PAUL WILSON is known around the world as 'the guru of calm'. As well as teaching meditation for almost 30 years, he's a businessman, lecturer and author. His books have sold over 8 million copies, and have been translated into 24 languages.

Other books by Paul Wilson:

The Quiet. Four simple steps to peace and contentment – without spending the rest of your life on a mountaintop.

For the whole story on meditation practice – from Day One to Enlightenment – look into Paul Wilson's book, *The Quiet*.

It's for everyday people who lead a non-stop life, but who long for the peace of mind, clarity of thought, and escape from the tensions of the modern world that traditional meditation offers.

The Quiet distils most of the major meditation approaches into a single, easy-to-understand practice that works.

And works much faster than you've been led to expect.

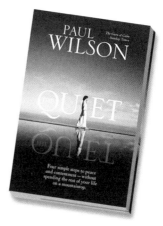